In Beauty Bright

In Beauty Bright

GERALD STERN

W. W. NORTON & COMPANY

New York • London

For information about permission to reproduce selections from this book,
write to Permissions, W. W. Norton & Company, Inc.,
500 Fifth Avenue, New York, NY 10110

For information about special discounts for bulk purchases, please contact
W. W. Norton Special Sales at specialsales@wwnorton.com or 800-233-4830

Manufacturing by Courier Westford
Production manager: Anna Oler

Library of Congress Cataloging-in-Publication Data

Stern, Gerald, date.
In beauty bright / Gerald Stern. — 1st ed.
p. cm.
ISBN 978-0-393-08644-7 (hardcover)
I. Title.
PS3569.T38881I5 2012
811'.54—dc23
                              2012015261

W. W. Norton & Company, Inc.
500 Fifth Avenue, New York, N.Y. 10110
www.wwnorton.com

W. W. Norton & Company Ltd.
Castle House, 75/76 Wells Street, London W1T 3QT

1 2 3 4 5 6 7 8 9 0

For my friends in Pittsburgh—during the dark time.

CONTENTS

Part I

Part II

Part III

Acknowledgments

Poems in this volume have appeared or will appear in the following journals.

The Antioch Review: "Against Whistling," "February 22," "Stoop"

American Poet: "Eastside"

The Cortland Review: "Thoreau's Metaphor," "Like Fools," "I Who Lifted a Car," "Gracehoper," "Garnish," "Stern's Cigars with Sholem Alechim"

Five Points: "Casals," "Domestic," "Frogs"

The Georgia Review: "For Beauty's Sake," "Immigrants"

Great River Review: "Broken Pipes," "Sugar," "Angel," "Lupe," "Blue Intact," "Died in the Mills," "Rosenblatt," "Angel of Death"

IWW Journal: "Frick"

Massachusetts Review: "Kafeteria," "Norman Riding"

The New Republic: "Dumb"

The New Yorker: "The Crossing," "Spring," "Dream IV," "Independence Day," "Nietzsche"

Organica: "Yellow Moon," "Rapture," "The Frick Mansion"

Poetry: "Leaves," "The Name," "In Beauty Bright," "Journey"

Poetry International: "Israel Grossman," "Donkey"

Poets.org: "Books"

Poem-A-Day: "Magnolia"

Smartish Place: "26 Vandam," "The Two Pyrenees"

The Threepenny Review: "Eleanor"

World Literature Today: "Sinai," "Goat"

"Broken Glass" appeared in *New Jersey Noir* edited by Joyce Carol Oates, published by Akashic Books, 2011

"Stoop" appeared in *Best American Poetry 2010*, edited by Amy Gerstler and David Lehman, published by Scribner Poetry, 2010.

"Dream IV" appeared in *Best American Poetry 2011*, edited by Kevin Young and David Lehman, published by Scribner Poetry, 2011.

"Casals" appeared in *Pushcart Prize XXXIV: Best of the Small Presses*, edited by Bill Henderson, published by Pushcart Prize Fellowship, 2012.

In Beauty Bright

Part I

February 22

Reading a Japanese novel during the one day of
sunshine following a week of rain, my daughter-in-law
going to the post office for the new stamps
and on her way home though it was winter and
bitter weather was on the way she found a
buttercup which meant, she said, the arctic
ice cap was melting and it was getting warmer
except we couldn't resist it and we walked
back through the streaks of ice and the mud for buttercups
are varnished, and we adore them, though we mostly
live in fear and, for that matter, we crawled
back and on the way I smashed the knuckles
of my left hand on the blue stone wall
for Ronald Reagan and Donald Duck had made it
but neither had Scott Nearing or Emma Goldman,
talk about nincompoops, talk about birthdays.

Against Whistling

How we walked for an hour hunting for the right wall
and how we kicked our feet at last while singing "Summertime,"
and one of us had a harp and one a black potato
and our feet touched the grass which from the bridge above us
must have looked heavenly which it was all fall and how
we looked like birds perched, as they say, on the wire
only there were fewer of us given our size and species
though we communed and we partook, and there was even
a kind of sound come separately and come randomly
partly from the mouth and partly from the potato,
and we took at last to naming the separate grasses
which is the way it is beside walls and under wires,
and some of us grew so happy we started to whistle
which is always a bad thing for beaks and for potatoes
given how in abandonment your eyes might be closed
and the horror of eagles might come down upon you.

Stoop

While on a stoop and eating boiled beef
and while my hands are dripping with horseradish
and while a crescent moon reflects itself
in one of the windows on Sixth Avenue
near what used to be the great Balducci's
across from the woman's prison and the library,
though truth the sky is blue so it is probably
April and it's probably twenty, thirty
years ago, and I was studying women's
shoes before the long point killed the two
end toes the same time I was killing time
before the meeting at the Waverly
inside a window as I recall for I had a
burden then and I was given to meetings
like that though even then I knew what it was
like to be free of burdens for I was part
mule, wasn't I, therefore I knew what freedom
was and I am mule to this day and carry a
weight, and I will to the grave—you will see me
put it into the hole first, it is so cumbersome,
with ears the color of the sun and compromised
by wings, which I am too, and there's one mule
I knew in the late '30s whose name was Molly,

alas, not Sal, and she wasn't stupid and she was
hardly stubborn and she loved apple trees
and she was wise and loving, above rubies.

Broken Pipes

There were plenty of broken pipes in the ceiling
and there were watery maps and such reminiscent of
the places he wandered through though once it was
the wallpaper made him stare, both that and the stains,
and this time there was a nose you couldn't miss,
you had to look at the funnies a hundred years ago
to see it and sometimes it still shows up in the flesh
when it is a finger or a fist although it
is a peninsula the likes of Italy
attached to a body at least the likes of Asia;
and sometimes it was a mock-tragic for tears
coasted down just such a nose and it was the pipes
themselves that caused the sadness, caught as they were
between two states; and that for him was enough
of Art to make him dream when he loaded the furnace
or turned the card in the window so the horse
could stop betimes surrounded by steam and covered
in frozen lather there on a hill across from
a woods in the Year of Your Lord, ridiculous.

Aliens

How on the river the loosestrife has taken over,
and how at the wedding there were spaghetti straps
and one or two swollen bellies, and the judge who
married them was wearing red sneakers and he was
altogether a little pompous, and how the
Guatemalans have moved into the borough
and they are picked up in front of the Flower Mart
sitting by the ice machine and there the
bargaining takes place and both sides love
light maybe because of the glittering
between the trees and locked inside the droplets,
and what the swollen river is up to and how
New York City is stealing the water and what,
with the weather events, there could be a failure
of one or more of New York's three earthen dams
or there could be a collapse of the steel tunnel
feeding the city, and what the language is
they argue with and whether it's under the table
the way they get paid or there are water-marked checks
with complicated deductions, and what the birds are
that eat the garbage and if a plastic milk box
turned upside down is not a good enough table

for coffee and donuts especially if the sugar
goes neatly through the holes and red plastic
makes music too and boots take the place of sneakers.

Like Fools

Like fools we waited to hear the tomatoes; we knew
what greenness meant on the vine and we were able
to bypass the peppers, green *and* red and stop at
the wall where nothing wet between the stones
gave them their shape to start with since they were mostly
flat and heavy and it was a vocable
so pure I almost froze and it was a guttural—
reaching out to the pines—the small rouge came from.

The Crossing

Not to forget that we had wooden guns once
just as the Germans did when they invaded
the Ruhr in 1936 and likewise
we abandoned wallpaper for paint
and there was an army of 500,000 monkeys
who carried wooden rifles over their heads
when they crossed the Delaware and how
the Hessians applauded and how George Washington
ordered grog for everyone there and since it
was a Christian holiday they built
the largest fire in New Jersey history
and even burned their beautiful boat whose curves
anticipated the helical waves and whose bottom
unfolded, as it were, or shot through water
something like a bottle or just skimmed
the surface like a stone and everyone sitting
stood up, not only Washington, and shouted
just above Trenton almost the shortest night
of the year and we spoke Deutsche and everyone hugged
the person to his right although the left was
not out of the question and we said, "Peace," we
always say it, the way they said it on the Rhine,
the way they said it on the Danube, and now the

Ohio, and now the Mississippi, the Susquehanna,
the Allegheny, hug your monkey, kiss
the nearest Romanian, kiss the nearest Greek.

Dumb

Fleabane again and I have another year
to take up its redness and what the wayside is like
with or without it and I have another year
to charge across the wooden bridge and shake it
again and take on the animals and fight
the stupid bikes and the bikers who ride across
with their legs spread out instead of walking their bikes
so we didn't have to be pushed against the rails,
they are so dumb and their bikes have so many dumb
and useless gears like a dumb idiot box
with 2,000 stations, only dumb ancient
boxing and ancient movies worth anything,
Jack Johnson or Marciano, even
Orson Welles too much, give me the unself-
conscious, Karl Malden or Jean Harlow,
for this is an old flower, it hates whatever
it wants to, it grows where it wants and it
loves goats because of their flattened eyes.

Rapture

It was a sound that had to exist by itself
unheralded and you sat in an unsprung
armchair with the wooden arms against
your chest, your heart skipping, your one thought
how you would get to the door or answer the phone,
and you said *love* and you agreed with yourself
though first it was *grief,* that stupid thing, and it was
ejaculation not your own that horrified
you and it was wistfulness for what would
one day be Disney but still was rat-ridden
and smelled of roach powder, and one of the radiators
was cold and one was so hot you burned yourself
at the wet socks but finally it was wind—
thank God for that—and while the building was bending
you leaned to make things right for that's what you do
at fifty miles per hour, and you said *rapture*
sometimes, as well as wistfulness, as well as love.

Casals

You could either go back to the canary
or you could listen to Bach's unaccompanied *Suites*
for which, in both cases, you would have the same sofa,
and you will be provided with a zigzag quilt to sleep
under and a glass-top table and great fury,
for out of those three things music comes;
nor should you sleep if even the round muscles
below the neck fall loose from their stringy moorings
for you would miss a sob and you would miss
a melody à la red canary
and à la white as well and à la canary,
perched, as the cello was, on top of a wooden box
and a small musician perched on top of the cello
and every night a church full of wild canaries.

Israel Grossman

Roses are mostly used on goat meat
and daisies on a piece of horse is finally
out of the question for who can fool whom while sitting
both either in or out, though it was sitting
out I spilled my flower over my horsemeat
and dug into my *frites* and there was sunshine
partout and I stared into the sun without
my glasses on my nose and with my eyes
open *à la* Huxley, who was teaching us
how not to go blind while living in California
with other English who were still that year
strewing roses; it was the Anno Domini
1955 and it was my cousin
Israel Grossman who for a flower went
to the stalls for lavender, preaching Huxley.

I Who Lifted a Car

My lips say the words too slow
but I am a drop in the bucket
and my body will never catch up
for I am going in reverse
and my slow mind has ruined me;

and pound for pound the fleabane
weighs the same as iron does
and one of my obsessions
is guessing the weight of bridges,
I who traveled by car,

and I can guess the weight
of a woman I am so good
though my lips say the words too slow
and my heart goes out to a woman,
I who drove a car.

But I am a drop in the bucket
and my body will never catch up
for I am going in reverse
and my slow mind has ruined me,
I who lifted a car.

Gracehoper

In the way Ovid lectured a green grasshopper
and all the grasshopper did was spit up tobacco,
in the way he begged for food for he was the first
bohemian, though he detested the brutal word
gracehoper, see James Joyce, and when two ants
ran around the corner when it was dinner
and how the gracehoper wept and it was cold
on top of the cold stone wall though dinner cost
at most say twenty cents, and how the ants
reasoned, and how the gracehoper, and what the stakes
were, and what the dream was, see Aesop.

Donkey

How God in three religions rode on his back
and one there was a festival and one he
dragged his feet on the ground until the dust
filled his sandals; and what we say is the mane
is *hogged* and you can fold your fingers around
and through and there are stripes that make him a zebra
though they are muted and he is a Chevy mostly
with a slant V6 and a tufted tail and a strip
in the center of the windshield which since it was
a type of truck it carried two enormous
pouches and died suddenly after a hundred
thousand miles or after a lifetime of burdens,
as a donkey does, first looking up for
it was his last piece of affection and he wanted
something more than he got though he was grateful,
and dying they *both* look up with grass in their teeth
or filthy handkerchiefs in their round metal mouths.

Garnish

How in the movie version the parsley religion
was all de Mille and Eddie Cantor jumping
between two dishes and making eyes in his
plaintive way and all there was to know
of taproots reaching down to hell and further,
since plants like that were only used for garnish,
though there was still an echo of the great rebirth
we sang and moaned about on Saturday morning.

Eleanor

She kept dropping her papers in front of no. 1 Fifth
which first started when she got out of a yellow DeSoto
and it was either a headwaiter or a doorman who rushed out
to pick them up and help her into the lobby
where Henry Wallace was waiting; and you should know
that though she hated his theory of eggs she sided
with him on other things, and it was Franklin
they discussed and it was the Age of the See-Saw
and the Cardboard Shoe, and both of them screamed with laughter
at Oysters Rockefeller, just imagine naming
food for *him,* how about calling soup
Cream of Carnegie, how about putting your canines
to work on Fried Frick or Chopped Harriman;
and God they hated Cardinal Spellman even before
he was the priest of war and of free busing,
and both of them loved the Buddha and listened together
to the sound of the Minetta creek suddenly surfacing
in the lobby across the street—no. 2—and they stood
back to back to see who was taller; and everywhere
in America boys of fifteen read her column
before they read the Funnies and put her picture
beside the one of their maternal grandmother's
though girls were more wary—except a few—and Adlai
loved her, and Harry, and Lyndon—and in the church

of the Ascension in front of the John LaFarge
or back of the sculpted angel she shook hands
and half bent down the way a tall woman does
to kiss someone; it could be any century
and it could be her friend or a loving stranger,
a former slave—or a boy of fifteen.

Leaves

He was cleaning leaves for one at a time
was what he needed, and a minute before the two
brown poodles walked by he looked at the stripped-down trees
from one more point of view and thought they were
part of a system in which the dappled was foreign
for he had arrived at his own conclusion and that was
for him a relief even if he was separated,
even if his hands were frozen,
even if the wind knocked him down,
even if his cat went into her helpless mode
inside the green and sheltering Japanese yew tree.

Sugar

How when I cut the giant Norway maple down
the first warm day the stump was covered in sap
and I ended up stuffing Russian sage
into my Polish nose and waving medicine
down and around the stump which in this case
was more like grass than it was a bush I picked
the other side of the bridge so I could consider
the other side of beauty for a while,
though when I saw the maggots all I could think of
was dead flesh and maggot therapy
and how the maggots stink and struggling bees
swimming in the syrup came up for air from
time to time but it was murder there
and there was murder everywhere and stumps
galore and broken this and that and smashed
everything I was supposed to venerate.

Two Graces

There were three but two were all I knew
and one was at least a head taller and if
their writing was different they came from different sides
of the same mountain or for that matter a street,
and it was as if the one sang low and the other
shrieked almost but that wasn't true they both
either hummed or sang soprano "Deep River" and ate
a fish soup there on the corner, and one of the two
grew up in the Bronx and one on 86th Street
not far from Central Park, and one was a free-
thinker of the kind in Union Square
they stood on boxes with a flag protecting them
and one went to a progressive school and studied
Scotch-Irish songs by traveling through the mountains
on a bike and visiting schools and jails
and one could never finish her studies but listened to
voices here and there and they both loved their
fathers who were always busy and one had
one of the first bat mitzvahs in New York City,
the other finally gave it up in Vermont
I think by swaying and fasting every autumn, and
if you went by the crow and the compass they finally
lived a few blocks from each other and at the windows
they sang and wrote and only by studying rain

and what came after were they able to know
one another or only by walking under
the Washington arch, or sitting on the benches
smoking and reading—and one thing more, they were
together in Houston once, thousands of miles
from Greece, I saw them, thousands of miles
likewise from the chess players at the confluence
of 4th and MacDougal; rain nourished them
going east and west on 8th and one more thing,
one of them trespassed on the White House lawn,
for which she was gravely lectured to and fined,
and one of them sat in a window on Sixth Avenue
wearing glasses and writing in a notebook,
and all this was south of 14th Street where
heads were regrown and wings grew out of shoulder blades
there was such glitter there, especially in April,
and shoes were given away, that was the key
to everything, a pile of shoes almost like a
mountain, certainly a hill, and there was a
river in which they swam, it goes underground
and you can reach it from a few of the lobbies,
and I have their photos on my walls, including
their shadows and once in a while when I go to dust them
some blue is hanging from the glass that might

not have been there the day before though it was
only a photo and it would have had to come
more than eighty miles, a hundred the clerk from
Triple A says, ninety to be exact,
some days when the wind is loud and unpredictable.

Spring

The road the road just south of Frenchtown the poem
the one by Mordecai the river the river the
one on my left if I am traveling north the
car a box with wires loose on top of my
left leg the radio fine the light behind
behind the clock not working the rose so dead
I am ashamed the crows too shiny their feathers
too wet the cliff on my right too red the blood
the blood of an animal, a skunk, they bleed
and stink, they stink and bleed, the monkey on top
of me, a New World monkey, not a howler,
an organ-grinder monkey, a capuchin,
his small red hat is on my head and he's
on my back, he's dropping orange peels down my
neck, March 22nd on the Delaware River.

Angel

It makes no sense to act like a stork or a shorn
poodle beside the which my muck is deep
enough that I could have the problem anyhow,
my left shoe either lost or ruined, or take
a huge grocery store at eight a.m.
and how you had to fight the wind to get there
and walk down a steep grass hill and under pine trees
dreaming of your first good cup and hating
whatever form the angel you hate comes in
or take a gang of dogs or a crazed Chevy.

Sinai

No one thought of naming his dog Sinai
for fear of offending the mountain, given how dogs
whimpered and growled outside the tents, their ribs
glistening in the fire, their tongues dripping
oh centuries before we clothed them and let them sleep
on our mattresses and named them Miriam and even
in one case I know Moses, more for his croupy
bark than anything else, for he was the one
that had the problem—though there were other mountains
and one was named Chicora after the poem
I wrote in 1944 though there was
never a dog by that name and that was a mountain
you ran up, it was so perfect, and at the top
above the chained-down cabin the stunted trees
bowed and groveled for they were dogs, and Sinai,
since she was not Misty and not Lucille, just whistled.

Domestic

It was as if his gills were going in and out
and there was a croaking noise he made that scared her
almost to death he imitated while lying
under her heavy salty blanket she pulled
up to his neck and tucked in at his sides
for she was going to read a little afterwards
and put her glasses on that perched on the edge
of her English nose and held her head in her hand
while he took in, for a second only, the streaks
of lightning mixed with the moonlight as if one brightness
was not enough, two gods he thought, and how the
river would smell tomorrow as he swam over
the greasy rocks and she would take him again
in her brackish arms that more than reading and more than
music it was she overcame her sorrow,
and that is why her elbows were sore and the rotten
underwater steps gave way and love
rushed into her mouth and mercy broke over her head.

I Caused His Death

What does it mean when only two people know the joke
or only two are left of the hundreds who used to roar
at the punch line, or only one slave was left in what
used to be the South though he was living in a suburb of
Washington called Rat Hill, or only twenty tiny insects
out of thousands and millions can recognize blue and are thus
eaten or drowned or beaten down by an angry walker
or a desperate on his way up a beaten-down towpath
watching the last iris and listening to turtles jump
into the water at rabbit speed or hare, or
that of the insects, nothing was seen of their love bites
not done in hatred nor even in hunger nor was there
much recorded of what was a car crash in Kennywood
or kisses on the lawn of the Pennsylvania College for Women
called PCW those years during the long afternoon
in Georgia where after sitting with a heavy wool blanket
around his knees in spite of the heat and the heavy
soup he ate Franklin Roosevelt suddenly died there.

Dream IV

I am so laden I grieve at 3 a.m.
over two parking spaces I could have claimed
or am fully frightened in a basement room choosing
a Nobel laureate among the nine Israelis
upstairs, especially when their phone call says
you don't have anything to be frightened of; nor would
I choose a Jubu, nor would I choose someone
with a ring in her tongue for it says in Numbers that
tin coated with silver is against the law
of mixing metals, such as we can't cook peppers
in a steel pot for steel is what we put
in a horse's mouth and what we make swords of
by dipping iron in oxide in the first place,
though it was no accident deliberately tipping wood
or fusing, as they did, Jewish and German
genius and German and Jewish chemicals
underground, and in the desert; I say fuck you
to fusion and I say let them fight with iron,
better with bronze, or better yet with wood,
or air, oh let them fight with air, drop air
from B100s, consider it, Kissinger.

Zikel

While he lay there thinking of his name
and read with his finger, and while his sister cooked
he touched his forehead with a burnt-out match,
one of the things he did, and he remembered
the bones returning to life and the little car
that went sideways he called his chariot;
and he was angry when they touched his hump
or even bewildered, and one rat patted him
on top of his head, for he was small though he was
at least forty, closer to fifty, the same height
as his cousin once removed who lived in a building
the next one over and had a voice that registered
the same soprano though *his* was more nasal and trapped
in the narrow cave between the bed and the window
in a child's chair between two rivers, both of them
full of tears and cries of horror and sledges
dragging blankets across the desert and gods
with curly beards and oversized eyes he hid from,
the cousin he loved and always kissed when he saw him.

26 Vandam

His room of choice was always up five flights
and always past the Chinese mother who played
on strings when he went by and hid the money
in one of the three or four dresses she always wore then;
and it was clouds he thought of for he was through
with birds who interrupted him with their plunging,
sometimes even their screaming; and there was a window
through which he shouted things and there was a moon, there
always is, though he preferred the dark, knowing
what light is; and he was given to falling just as
others were given to rising; and as for the sky
I swear there was snow on his blanket but where it came from
and where the poem on the table came from and what
went back thirty years he gave up knowing
nor was there much reason left in arguing.

The Two Pyrenees

There is no shame in singing together, the first
Neanderthals did it in both Pyrenees, although
the theory that they were acting like frogs might be
as wrong as right—I prefer it were wolves
if such their throats were they could howl that way
for there is no proof that frogs were ever connected
to moonshine—moonlight—but wolves they always were—
they are—and as for those thickset people I love
so much I know they had to sing to the moon—
I sing myself behind my fronds, my porch,
my metal table, something to go with the sighing
of the coconuts in love with the bleeding
hearts and bar scotch in a cardboard cup
to keep the cold out for flowing water is
everywhere to keep the plants from freezing
and I am doing it for you, abominable friends.

Lupe

Papa Luigi was the name you were trying to
remember and how slowly he came down from his
house to denounce the American photographers,
or it may be sitting all day with the wolf while we called
his owner over the only working telephone—
as if it were a holiday—then resting my
feet in salt for a week and eating fish
with my hands, or it may be the two of us singing
Bella Napoli, for there was a spray
that mixed with tears to prove all water is one
in sight of the great volcano where I kissed her
among the noisy oars and the stale sandwiches.

Yellow Moon

There was an expert at conversion who fought
his audience for hours he was so keen on
John—and Paul—and it was a field of recalcitrant
daisies he thought he was preaching to or sometimes
a houseful of small Rhode Island Reds—he told me,
oh, 1947—but it was a weed patch of
filthy hecklers outside a depraved theater
on 42nd Street and he had a Bible
he slammed against his leg and fists like stone
he longed to smash against the Jews and atheists
who laughed at him, but don't forget conversion,
say how a laugh turns into tears, say how a
rat grows a fluffy tail and stands up to
crack a nut, so dear, and when I lay in
bed in Florida with a yellow streetlight
on top of me and couldn't manage the blinds
I had to convert it to a yellow moon
a mile or so away from my bed and lie there
among the burnt-out wax and cold noodles,
easy since my back hurt from walking and easy
since there were some dried-up apples on my table,
and I could thereby go from century to century
and live in a sweater that smelled like a spring lamb
since I had gone before to a yellow moon.

Frogs

The part that we avoided was not the heart
but what we called the pouch, for it still swelled
or seemed to and there was plenty of horror cutting
into what made the music or at least
the agency you might call it, and more than one of us
retched and as you know, that can become
contagious—think of a roomful of pouches exploding
think of the music on a summer night
with no one conducting and think of how warm it might be
and how love songs may have gotten started there.

In Beauty Bright

In beauty bright and such it was like Blake's
lily and though an angel he looked absurd
dragging a lily out of a beauty bright store
wrapped in tissue with a petal drooping,
nor was it useless—you who know it know
how useful it is—and how he would be dead
in a minute if he were to lose it though
how do you lose a lily? *His* lily was white
and he had a foolish smile there holding it up like
a candelabrum in his right hand facing the
mirror in the hall nor had the endless
centuries started yet nor was there one thorn
between his small house and the beauty bright store.

Part II

Journey

How dumb he was to wipe the blood from his eye
where he was sucker punched and stagger out
onto the plaza blind. He had been waiting
all night for the acorn moon and eating pineapple
topping over his ice cream and arguing
either physics or philosophy. He thinks,
at this late date, it was the cave again
throwing a shadow, although it may have been
only some way of reconciling the two
oblivious worlds, which was his mission anyhow—
if only there was a second moon. He had a
kind of beard and though he could practically lift
the front end of a car and was already
reading Blake, he had never yet tasted honey.

Kafeteria

I who kame late to the kafeteria
at least had one or two tastes of
apple kake and milky koffee and ah
prunes and the jus of lemons in a krakked
kommercial saucer—I guess a bowl—women
yes, with hats with feathers but mostly men;
and walked on a broad pavement karrying
a gym bag probably long before you strapped
yourself down like a walking ape and certainly
I touched everything touchable and stopped
in front of a dummy I had fallen in love with
and kried myself silly over her helplessness
an hour or so before my maiden speech
just north of Fourth where through the books I wandered
one door after another just to the west
of Klein's Department Store, a small flag
for kover, an orange krate for a stage, a
skornful audience, Amerika in hell again.

Books

How you loved to read in the snow and when your
face turned to water from the internal heat
combined with the heavy crystals or maybe it was
reversus you went half-blind and your eyelashes
turned to ice the time you walked through swirls
with dirty tears not far from the rat-filled river
or really a mile away—or two—in what
you came to call the Aristotle room
in a small hole outside the Carnegie library.

Goat

The two of them argued who would take the head
and who would take the feet the way they fought
over whether the breathing stopped before or after
the bleeding began, though it could have been a goat,
the way they shouted, and they could have petted the stiff
hair between the horns as he was screaming,
or they could have stopped to argue about the haunches
and who to consult if the neck was already broken.

Stern's Cigars with Sholem Aleichem

Lunchtime they argued over the plots and sometimes
one of them read a passage with a heavy, say,
Polish accent and for a minute they were like
the men, although they never pounded the table,
and later the fumes either made their eyes water
or made them dream, though their fingers were independent
and clever; and there was a large white sink in which
they scrubbed their yellow hands nor did they have
too far to go nor did they work too long there,
and those who married, as like as not married downstairs
or in the yard, if it was warm, among the
flowers they had no names for they gathered and wore
like feathers in their curly uncut hair.

Magnolia

The mayor, in order to marry us, borrowed
a necktie from a lawyer which, on him,
looked stupid and kept his eye on a red pigeon
which somehow got in to coo her disappointment,
if only for the record, though one of the two
witnesses who kicked the red got only what
she deserved and that was that, except that the
rain cooed too, but we didn't give a shit
for we had a bed, for God's sake, with two tin buckets
of blossoms waiting for us; and someone there
of Greek persuasion enacted the dancing though somewhat
lickerish and turned to reading the names of the dead
from World War I the other side of the bandstand
but we didn't care nor did we know her name
nor where she came from or what the necktie or what
our love had to do with it anyhow, mostly nothing.

Blue Intact

I looked at the earth with drunken moonlit eyes
and thought I had discovered the blue intact
which gave me such pleasure before my sleep and let me
open and close one eye the while I wandered
before I fell into my own hole there
chewing and rechewing the blue earth,
loving and reloving as the moon does there
dark behind the cloud, then reappearing,
worrying over its own huge islands as the earth does there.

Died in the Mills

Then, fifty dollars for a Hungarian
say a black dress to go to the funeral
and shoes with soles for the three oldest, that leaves
a dollar fifty for the feast but I'd say
what a dollar was worth then you could have
a necktie if you wanted and paprikash
for twenty or thirty and strudel with apples and nuts
and violins—he favored the violin—
and it is not just poets who love meadows
and take their sneakers off and their socks to walk
on the warm rocks and dip their tender white feet
in the burning freezing water and then bend down
precariously to pick up a froglet and sight
the farthest lonely tree and note the wind
moving quickly through the grasses their last summer.

Rosenblatt

The most revolting thing of all was carrying
a suitcase through the gate for that was mixing
your journeys, even wearing an overcoat
or socks—with clocks—inside your shoes was stupid,
but nothing compared to a suitcase, amazing compartments
for matching neckties and handkerchiefs, and one
for underwear and one for toilet articles
which when it was forced open—for who had such
a tiny key—there was your name burned in
the leather, nor did the scalloped bottles spill,
dear Rosepetal, son of the Hamburg kosher fishmonger.

Norman Riding

All that morning he had a merciful attitude
and this is what made him remember the swamp maple
that blocked the sunlight from his kitchen window
though it was idiotic to remember a tree that
anyhow labored over its own death and hung on
like some mad ninety-five-year-old on pills;
and the crash itself was gracious for the tree
could still bend, and when it cracked a hundred
things went flying and he who rode it he went
flying too, with bladed saw, his two arms
either cheering or keeping the branches away
from his sawdust glasses, all of which enlightened
his whole yard and set his other trees free;
though how pathetic a giant is on the ground
covered with ants he hates and here and there
a squirrel or a bird ignoring him as it nibbled
and gobbled and drank and spit and chewed as if
they all were eating and drinking at a funeral,
only the corpse was lying dead in the dirt
with his skin peeling and his hair blowing and his mouth
opening on its hinges, the great creases
clarified by the sun, the song insane.

June Through September

Tomatoes hung from a stick
and marigolds because it was the custom
and something gold was bouncing on a leaf
to get at the seeds in one of the buried faces;
and something besides the starving insects
was drilling madly into the purple cups
and they ignored each other though they had heartbeats
only a yard apart;
and none of us once gave up though it was getting
dark and one of the candles was spitting light
for we had run out of soup and Wittgenstein
was getting boring now and we were drowning in
wax and it was finally time again
to talk about murder in one form or another,
given how close we were to Philadelphia,
and how the wind carried the cries and moans
for fifty-six miles up Route 95 and then
up 29, and what we did with that
either as birds or insects, June through September.

Iberia

I have been here so long I remember Salazar
and how he tortured my four main poets in Portugal
with his "moral truth and patriotic principles,"
and fatherless Coughlin and all the old bastards
that stretched in one great daisy chain from the coast
of California east and east to New York and
London and thence across Eurasia to God knows
what small moral and patriotic islands
so listen to me for once and hate for good
all moral islands, and if you haven't done so
already add my Pessoa to your Lorca.

Independence Day

There were packs of dogs to deal with and broomsticks
whacking rubber balls and everyone stopping for
aeroplanes and chasing fire engines
and standing around where sidewalks on hills turned almost
level, and horses and horseshit, and ice in the cellars;
and Saturday I wore a dark suit and leaned
against my pillar and Sunday I put on a necktie
and stood in front of a drugstore eating a Clark Bar.
The 4th of July I stayed in my attic resting in
filthy cardboard and played with my bats, I stretched
their bony wings, and put a burning match
to the bundle of papers, especially to the ropes
that held them together and read the yellow news
as it went up in smoke and spoke for the fly and raged
against the spider, say what you will, and started
my drive to Camden to look at the house on Mickle Street
and walked—with him—down to the river to skip
some stones, since Ty Cobb did it and Jim Thorpe did it
though it was nothing compared to George Washington
throwing silver dollars, and for our fireworks
we found some brown beer bottles and ran down 3rd Street
screaming, but he had to go back home and sit
in his rocking chair for there was a crowd of Lithuanians
coming and he was a big hit in Vilnius

the way he sat in his mound of papers and gripped
the arms, though I was tired of Lithuanians
who didn't know shit, not to mention Romanians,
to pick a country out of a hat—or I was
just tired and Anne Marie was right, I shouldn't
be driving at night, I should be dead, I don't
even know how to give instructions, I don't even know
my rabbi's name—she and her motorcycle—
imagine them speaking Babylonian over
my shoe box—imagine them throwing flowers—fleabane,
black-eyed Susans, daisies—along with the dirt.

The Name

Having outlived Allen I am the one who
has to suffer New York all by myself and
eat my soup alone in Poland although
sometimes I sit with Linda he met in Berkeley
or San Francisco when he met Jack, the bread
just coarse enough, the noodles soft but not
thin and wasted, and not too salty the way the
Chinese farther down sometimes make them, the
name still on my mind whatever the reason for
mystery, or avoidance, though rat Netanyahu
and pig that swings from a needle or lives in some
huge incubator, they do darkness where there
was light, the *name* hates them, the *name*
in hiding, the *name* with a beard, and Linda she
loves the *name* though she invokes her Christ
as Jack her lover and tormentor did and
taught her to do though it is too easy, that,
it troubles me but what can I say, what *should* I
say while we walk north on the right-hand side,
past the pork store and the hardware store, me lecturing
on Logos (my God) and what-not Hebrews and Greeks
where Allen and I once kissed, Jack in the sun now.

Broken Glass

Broken bottles brought him to Mickle Street
and pieces of glass embedded in the mud
to Whitman's wooden house across the street from
the Church of the Most Unhappy Redeemer for when
it was too quiet he broke another bottle
and he collected his glass in a paper bag
and when he was *verloren* he cut himself
though just as like he cut himself on a wall
while doing an exercise to stretch the tendons
so he could get rid of the numb and burning feeling,
or sometimes he sat on a hydrant and once on a bench
with drooping slats so when the slats gave his back
also gave and feeling came back to his foot
as it came back to Whitman when he sat
on the orange rush seats or rocked in his chair between
the visits and loved the hollyhocks that grew
in the cracks and for a nickel the whole republic
would turn to broken glass as Oscar insisted.

The Frick Mansion

Figuring up what you might call an exchange,
and only for a painting but not counting
the claim of a share in the sixty rooms or counting
a share of the inflation compared to the mean
reduction of so many bodies in such a heavy
cardboard box or two, I'd say three hundred
fifty to seven hundred fifty, taking in
a complicated system of matching death payments
with the cost of buying or stealing, or I'd say
three hundred dead Slovaks for one Caravaggio.

Max Factor

Whither thou goest, I will go, sayeth Ruth,
and Naomi sayeth nothing for see one you
see them all and picture me at a small
vanity, my legs are squeezed together,
and I am constructing one of my utopias
with one of the English philosophers in mind
and I am overcome by powder reading the
secrets of the Eastern Star for which my
mother labored as one of the five sacred.

Soll Ihr Gornisht Helfen
Nothing Will Help

Some Austrian Jew or other who dipped his head
in Christian Water so he could get a job
in Wien or some such place, whose cousins galore
never dipped, never stripped,
for they were Jewish through and through
and carried their suitcases into the blue
whatever the gossamer gowns *they* wore
though it didn't help a bit,
all that shit
for he had a leather suitcase too,
Austrian Jew.

Voltage

I don't know one thing from another but I
think the one on the left is a television wire
and the one on which the blue jay jumps is electric
though how they plan the flow to go up the bricks
or right across the yard it's one of the secrets
and I am learning something about high voltage
and insulation and the different kinds of
poles and I do like the small and crooked ones;
and when the wires were put in conduits I even
grieved for I like torture to be in the open
and cruelty, or indifference, not to be buried
like oral agreements in some small living room,
and I am beginning even to like Verizon and
Sprint, loose and hanging multiple wires
every which way, for in a decade from now
I could grow nostalgic for the metal
footrests and the signs we nailed on poles
for parties and sales or the uphill walk
in Nebraska underneath the endless rows
and what remained of the messages, a cry
from red Eugene or red Emma, Mumford
swallowing his sword, never a word
from Stockholm, though a little later the rodents
made their speeches and got their millions, and those

were masters of the underground pipes and conduits
and loved their secrecy and spoke with accents
here and there and were invited to castles
and added fees to their prizes lovingly
and watched their backs of course because you never
know when the hot blue murderous currents will get you.

For D.

Let not a grocery bag of bloody napkins come between us.
Or a floor covered with cigarette butts and dirty underwear
or an alcoholic son or a paper with your
instructions regarding the upper and lower keyholes.

. . .

Let me not be a part of yet another creative narrative.

. . .

Come now the love.

. . .

Come now the two-inch predator wasp dragging a huge insect
over the rocky sidewalk into his dark hole under the porch.

. . .

Come the bees now clinging to flowered curtains.

Thoreau's Metaphor

His metaphor was of the white maples yielding
sugar and what the sugar camp was like
and the sumac sprouts;

and of twigs wrapped in the daintiest packages
and freight paid.

Mine is of the policeman following me in Beechview
thirty years ago from street to street up
one steep hill and down another, my car going
slower and slower, stopping once even—for a second—
so I could look at a piece of paper and circle
back to where I started with the dead bird I smelled in the
    woods.

Mine is of the dead bird.

Slow to Learn

Sarcasm came down on me like red dust and
contempt like the street lamps they lit after school
so we could find our own way home in the dark.

I lived in fear that I would lose my colored bookmark and
shame at the laughter coming from the front seat of the Pontiac.
And I hate that I was the truest of all balloons
you beat for the sweet and delicate things inside.

But I'm fed up with bitterness

and I learned from Brecht that anger at injustice
makes your voice hoarse, and hatred of vileness
distorts your features, but I already knew it.

Hyena

Richard Nixon

The fact that his front legs were longer than his rear
or I should say his arms, it made it possible
while hunching over—shouldering—to give the
two-handed V for Victory signs and do his
smiling just before he boarded the airplane,
Stupidity I, but made it hard to drink
his tea unless he doubled his wrist but such
it is for hyenas when they leave the capital
and such it is they grin—I saw his death
in Chicago over four hundred television stations,
eating ice cream and waiting; there was only
one poet in the whole airport—going from
station to station crying "asshole" and watching
his friend Clinton drop a tear for him
in 1993, and ah, you didn't have
Hyena to kick around much any longer.

Rage

I lost my rage while helping a beetle recover
and stood there with precision, balancing
grass with stone and lifted my stick to show
how dirt holds us up and what is indifferent and what
their music could be and what the whistling train,
according to childhood and ecstatic age.

A Hole

If they spent three days discussing a hole,
and if it existed while they were asleep or they were
in Guadalajara and the hole was in Baja,
or did it exist because they said it existed
or thought about it even, what were the chances?
And wasn't it a hopeless hole and didn't it
smack of infantile knowledge, Bishop Berkeley
lore, those screaming monkeys in the forest?
Though didn't the discussion exist because it was on
the closed-in porch while she was in the kitchen
cooking and cleaning, making black tea mostly,
who when she walked onto the porch she said
the hole existed since she was the enemy
of holes that didn't exist, or roses, or monkeys
such as the howler and such as the spider, but he,
the one who championed tinkering, was a well-known
criminal in Paris and a Jew for a while and a Catholic
priest who stole men's clothing when he was
twenty-two, for which the humming bird rages
and maples weep in the fall and black ants labor.

Too Late

Too late now to look for houses
to give readings, to flirt, to eat blueberries,
to dance the polka—or just to be in the
Serbian-American club in Duquesne
near that horrible McKeesport, near
that horrible Kennywood Park, and take
a sip, a bite, and half fall off my
stool, and grab her and whirl for fifteen
straight, or just to feel her breasts
against me and to loosen my tie,
my short and flowered tie, or just to
drive home slowly, sometimes even
on the streetcar tracks themselves,
that 68 trolley I loved so much, the
love seats and the rattling glass windows.

The Farm

It is more like a wall or the steps you fell down
grabbing the air while learning from *The Nation*
and turning purple how agribusiness is stealing
the smell of oats or the wet bottom layer of hay where
the pitchfork entered; and you will never again,
for you were a fool, pull up the stiff blankets
the end of August or ride a Sicilian donkey
while playing croquet, or sit there eating warm hash
and brushing the flies away, or just for starters,
drive your car in the ruts and keep the angry
bushes away from your window for you were a fool
because you wouldn't sleep on a lumpy bed and worship
a beam of sunlight and give yourself to the gnats
who beat their paper wings for that kind of worship.

Love

I loved your sweet neck but I loved your shoulder blades more
and wondered whether I should kiss your cheek first
or your hair for I was watching carefully, and
sitting on the edge of the tub I thought of
the three great places, namely the three gardens
of Eve, Gypsy Rose Lee, and Mrs. Bloom
lately of Auschwitz, though there are others, oh
there are others, but show me the two hands concealing
love and you have the whole history of the human race there.

Nostalgia

Stalin comes to mind who tried to destroy
everything they remembered, including the tree
they ate from, green delicious, including the store
they stole from after school, including the water
they leaned their foreheads on the moss for and even
the blue stone that once diverted the river
and by so doing came loose and was for the two
long months a dangerous step, but not the bulldozer.

For Beauty's Sake

For beauty's sake, among the rusted diesel
some goldenrod, the lowest living form
of goldenrod, not even the allergies
grew there—compare it to the hotel you lived in
that stank of urine on 8th Street near the rats, or
compare it to Norman's apartment in East New York,
the mattress against the wall, really the box spring
underneath he lowered with one hand and
threw a pillow down on and slept with his foot,
as I recall, engaging a chair leg and how
he lifted it up in the morning and straightened it out
so he could walk there and so it wouldn't fall
on him and his computer—for beauty's sake
he did that and he walked out to see the changes,
he did that every morning before he wrote his
thoughts down in his marbleized notebook and looked
up over the tallest ugliest buildings to find
some refuge from the sun, he and goldenrod.

The Farewell

For Philip Levine

Who can account for my hat, God save him, give him
a prize, bring him a goat; where are the bats
to go with the balls and where are the gloves, the webbed
and oiled and pocketed; where are the mothers
who waited for us when we got off the streetcars?
Where was the war? Why is there a basket of
softballs beside my wooden pig, and wasn't I
an expert at counting the troops on their side and ours?

What does it mean to march diagonally
the way the Americans did in Barcelona
on their way to the harbor where every woman
came out to show her gratitude and every
balcony was full, and every street
was covered in flowers, and horses and trucks were smothered
since grief is shown that way, and they may have sung
or they may have marched to the ships without a word
though mostly crazed and compromised for they were
communards of a sort among the ugly who
hated peasantries of any sort and
gave short shrift to grief, including the dead
softball team and the four broken gloveless fingers
among the stages of grief, even the songs
one of the stages since grief is a dead wolf

lying on its side and a bird eating
the black intestines—and the bird eaten—for they
have to die too, witness the smell in the woods,
witness the cat, witness Birdie her sticks up,
her eyes X's, witness the ghosts being lowered
seventy years later nor button nor regalia.

Part III

Nietzsche

You can say what you want but I love Nietzsche most
when he stood between the terrified horse and the coachman
and *intervened* though I have pity for his sudden
madness even if he hated pity for he was
human then nor could one word matter anyhow,
and when he went insane, as I understand it,
he suffered from shame and sadness in different cities
for which we have the very late letters his vicious
sister never burned, and though I know
it wasn't Heine or Émile Zola I thought
it had to be either Gogol or Dostoyevsky
who threw their arms around the bleeding horse;
and there is so much to say about him I want to
live again so I have time to study him,
for intervening is the only mercy left now,
as Grace walked on the White House lawn, as Daniel
broke the nose cones and burned the draft cards as if
those were the poems, not making up tunes to go
with a noisy furnace—it was for Nietzsche. Before
anyone was born I walked through the Armstrong tunnel
connecting one language to another, holding
a book in front of me and crowding the wall,
especially when I came to the curve so I could
live the *first* time, more or less, which when I

think of the working horse it was the bag
of oats, the blinders, the snorting, and the complex of
leather straps, but what wouldn't I give today,
June eleventh, two thousand nine, to talk to
Stanley or, for that matter, Paul Goodman
or those who came before—could I be the one
who carries the smell of dead birds in his blood, and horses?

San Jose 1985

There was Laughlin weeping for Pound and me
explaining his paradise and Duncan loving me
from the second row and later giving me
a signed copy of his manuscript;
and I didn't know he was dying, and later at lunch
telling Laughlin I worked for his daddy in one of the
hearths; and he was still weeping at how they made
fun of blacks and Jews and Hunkies, their jokes
astounding; and there was no sulfur where they lived,
and he said Pound wouldn't listen and I spent the next day
walking up and down the streets there thinking
of the French and Spanish poets, to name just two,
and what their models were compared to ours
and how we lifted the cream from the dirty milk.

Sleeping with Birds

I have slept with a Crow and a Robin and it's
not easy, birds, nor going to the airport without
a passport nor singing for security
something out of Noël Coward and thus
proving you're English and telling them you're on the way
to catch a bird; but you had to take your shoes off
anyhow and they put a stick up your groin
and one down your throat and you made walrus noises
to show your suffering.
                                    And it was Crete
you traveled in and she had a withered wing
from being crushed by a horse when she was thirteen;
and what you remember is how she sobbed after
climbing into the bus and putting her suitcase
into the overhead bin, but I am conflating
trips and even conflating birds though this one
was named Mavis and she wrote long letters
for she was English, and her last name was Sparrow.

Immigrants

There was a rat I know who squeezed inside
the chest and since he was eating Russian newspapers
he broke the China to get at the words nor did he
care if it was Antwerp or Hamburg and that was
the chest we got to keep, the other was lost,
a thick cardboard with metal at the corners
and not one rat inside, though there had to be
insects with all that clothing, wherever it got to,
and there the papers were mostly in Polish, nor did it
matter we came with dollars and wrung our hands
and looked at the sky nor did our prayers matter
or any bargains we made in either language
nor that there was a brilliant blue diamond
wrapped in a sock for which we could have had
an indoor toilet, nor what we had for breakfast.

My Libby

I hung onto her likeness and centered it
but as far as the samovar
they threw it into the river
when they took a raft somewhere
or just they bought someone *else's* keepsakes,
and as far as the chest
of hand-sewn sheets and pillowcases
they set it on fire
and floated it into West Virginia
but I who came for the light
I learned to sing and put my back out of place
by reading on the floor
for I was either the first or second generation
depending on how you counted
and I could have once become a Quaker
and now I have to confess
that it was I who hung them up to dry
and folded them in the dark
for here you have to fight for life.

Eastside

We on the eastside—whatever city—we came
there first there was a river we hugged the water
we loved the restaurants and the library and the horses
you wouldn't know it now you have a chauffeur
we walked up the broken sidewalk we trusted the clock
we ran our sticks on the chain-link fences we even
planted a tree we watered it we even
pissed in the dark we ran to catch a streetcar
we threw our bottles over we sat against it
and sang I was Bing Crosby I loved you so
I started running halfway home I passed
a dog all by himself I passed a small
Mobil station I looked inside a Studebaker
I'd love to show you a cave I'd love us to sing
"Perfidia" here is a yellow 1920s
cast-iron Mack truck here is a tiny steam shovel.

86th Birthday at MacDowell

Why do you always climb an extra pair of stairs
to get to a good light and why does all your pain—
speaking only of backaches—always show in your neck,
and do you think it only shows there or also under the pouch
of your left eye, and can't you just cut your neck off?

And what is the age of your fellow artists shrieking from
their crowded table and shouldn't I be working all day
with Allesandra changing words from thirty years ago
to make myself more musical and when will she be
done with Einstein's bastardly life and ready to give herself
to my fine animal, vegetable and human love songs?

Traveling Cages

Most of my money was on the gorilla though
the leopard tore his arm off at the shoulder,
but it was a question of cages
for a gorilla needed open spaces to move in;
and my loose change was on the birch tree
that it could bend in two without it cracking
in this colossal snow or that,
just as my dollars were on Bertrand Russell
who took his clothes off and changed bedrooms
whatever country he happened to be in,
though why I hardly know for we would bet
on anything; and one of my favorites
was odds and evens, whether the buildings
on 103rd between Broadway and Columbus
had five stories or six, but when it came
to the gorilla and the blood-soaked leopard's mouth
I stopped a minute to scream
at traveling cages and unlocked doors
and what the rules were concerning music
and where the elephant gun was kept
in one paralyzed dog-rearing dog-town or other.

Box

Oh and ah, how much I've wept
over the lost and useless things
and held my pillow against my throat
while the wind blew the feathers all but away,

but oh and ah, it isn't a waste
what I'll do in ten more days
here in my zone, whatever yours is,
whatever you do, the one astounding
thing now that the onions are in

standing on a box though everyone
I know is bicycling or running on the towpath
for now my subject is water, and will be
water again, though you would say
there are no leaves and even the sage
is dead and even the Chinese dogwood.

Effigies

Take a dog to the vet's, he knows what you're doing,
a cat becomes a muscle, she leaps from your arms
and oh, and ah, you won't kiss your dog
because of where his mouth was, and ah,
your cat has delivered a rat at your door
so lie down on the left side, or the right,
and let me find a place for my arm

for what can the police do
or the effigies floating over us
made of cloth and stuffed with cotton,

one only with a whistle,
one only with a sheet of white paper.

Angel of Death

Celan is not the only one for whom the
16th Psalm lay on his lips or more the
inside of his mouth or more the bone in his
second throat for which he drinks and he drinks though
there is no bone and there is no chicken now anywhere
nor is there one opossum left in whose wet
pouch a dead child lay too sick to move then;

and there was only one in Amsterdam then
who quarter-mongered you might say and ran
from house to house with a paintbrush and the red
smears by which you knew him stretching his arm
up and above and over the door on which the
light from a star guided Death as in Rembrandt
a black side curl reflected the light from Arcturus.

Plaster Pig

It didn't work that the bores I grew up with
smeared my door with lard
for I was enlightened and walked with the rest
in the mountains of Italy on Easter morning
and went to St. John's on Christmas Eve;
and neither does anyone I know
keep a plaster pig in his living room
for it is not what goes into the snout,
and you will forgive me
whether you like it or not
for wasn't it being *afraid* of the pig
that drove us there in the first place
and wasn't it God in the second,
and it had bristles in the third,
and the lungs were too small
and it was as smart as a fox terrier
and lived in shit.
And it turns wild in a second like nothing else
and someone once told me the male
has a cock that twists around like a corkscrew
and for those reasons I won't eat it.

Apt. 5 FW I

We return to the blood pudding
every chance we get
that every poet in Cracow
knows just as he knows the cabbage,
so fok the five flights
and the door to the roof
and the plaster ceiling since
my left arm hung down and scribbled
on the gray and green and yellow painted floor;
and there was a wind in the airshaft
and a red and blue beacon I said of Empire
that Schechter called the Divine Light
so give me back my Chinese landlady and my orange bathtub.

Counting

You remind me always it's thirteen years
though when I sit with my calendar or after
with just my fingers I can't remember or just
confuse myself by trying to put my things
 in order but I am almost always wrong
and I have to empty the room and pull the blinds down
and fold up the rug and sweep the floor
and put a wooden chair under the window
so I can think by squeezing the rungs until
the veins in my hands turn blue, for in the beginning
I climbed into your car and two weeks later
though neither of us gave it a thought we walked
across the street for breakfast where there was an ocean
nearby and that's the morning we started counting.

Art

I would carry my head in a basket and wait
at the doorbell for two full minutes while you fussed
upstairs with a lacquer and a final small touch
of red, or brown with red, or for an experiment
blue mixed in though it never worked and you'd
have to bend to see, blue maybe on the eyes
for delicacy, or blue between the breasts,
for it will disappear when you fix your earring
and bend again to kiss my cheek and my ears,
red again, the dinner profound, four tablespoons
of salt and sugar mixed and spread on the paper
tablecloth for that is the way it started
forty thousand years ago and either a
straw or a broken pencil for we were in company
and though we didn't wear gloves our fingers were clean
and I blew into the straw for my first octopus.

Apt. 5 FW II

I practiced something, I'm sure of it,
though I didn't know its name or that there was
consistency and aggregation nor was it a
question of oxygen or standing there looking
at something blue and red but I forgot food
while *studying*, if that is the word, and when I
returned, if that is the word, I was delighted
with everything, though *anything* is more likely,
the mirror that lost its silver, the orange bathtub,
the heavy locks, the cracked tiles, the toilet;
a lighted shaft that it could have been the moon
or it could have been a spotlight
and I could have lain there for hours on my bed
going slowly back to sleep, no bitterness.

Creeley

For James Haba, creator of the Dodge Poetry Festival and its director
for its first twenty years

At Panther Valley, according to my notes,
and it says 10 p.m. which means the restaurant
was just about to close and you had to go
to the bar to get your pretzel,
though I forgot to note the year,
he sat in a booth by himself
and seemed to hate the general merriment
and either by way of bitterness or contempt,
or likely unbearable sadness,
he went out to swallow 2,000 stars
for it was he who hated the general merriment
and Bly and Stafford were sitting at the bar
and Olds and Levine had come too late,
though they were part of the general merriment,
and they saw Creeley swallowing
the 2,000 stars for it was he who hated
the merriment and nothing I could do
could stop him from swallowing
even if we came to the same conclusions,
though I don't know what the year was.

Orangey

It's only when a chair appeared
outside my kitchen window
or the orange cat I hate
licking squirrel from his lips
holding his head up to catch the breeze
his tail lodged in the sky
walking later in front of the downtown cannon
with such arrogance you'd think
he was a city employee
handing out tickets or climbing
the stairs inside the old jail
free of the stupid blue jay,
home from fucking something,
his muscles loose and wandering,
his feet in felt slippers,
a Nazi if I ever saw one,
that I lay down on the straw
or even started to eat it
for I still had a choice I
thought, among the bovines,
in spite of my love of meat
and my addiction to shoes
orangey being only an
ugly figure, a type of

goat we tossed into the river
and washed our hands afterwards,
for it had nothing to do
with him or was it her or
even von Stein—or Ruskin—I'd
just as soon hang from a doorknob
for he had his own birdbath,
the feathers of a girl
partout, partout, Heraclitus
turning him back into mud
but orangey into fire,
waiting for water, ye birds,
chair in the air, huge cat
worried about the chair,
sleeping here and there.

The Lost Mountain

Those who live on government cheese and carry it
home from a church's back entrance in a bag to
hide the kind deed, you know how they
actually sneak away, for sneak can take a
dozen forms; and they can't understand
how the mountain of their dream delectable
once it was denuded it was denuded
forever; and the water stank and it will
take two hundred years to give the money back
for which they rub their eyes and scratch their webbed
hands, they whose children will never go to
the Latin schools of New Jersey, thus they will lose
the tongue and even the candles that lit up
the books at night, the rough fruit boxes against which
they might have scraped their knees, the lost mountain—
and cheese, with worms, what's going on, Abe Lincoln?

The Beginnings

I went back to the colorless ant which in
the beginning Drake and Margolis tell us swarmed
over each other's bodies which was their own
Beginnings; and the crows have theirs and they are
stuck with a name, that's why they talk, that's why
they rewrite their *Beginnings*, as in the beginnings
there were no murders or, in the beginnings there were
no trees; and nobody had an *Endings* though later
ants lived underground with millions of ladybugs
they enslaved just for the juices and swarmed
over the bugs and later on they ate them
though twice as fast as they did when they first swarmed;
and crows lived then in trees or you would say
they lived again and talked about it endlessly,
mostly their luck for they had the brains of humans
and they were thinking of tools but they were trapped
which made them furious but in the trees they argued
as if they were Greeks or they were Christians in Paris
or Jews living again in the 10th century
mostly in Spain in courts where they were doctors
and financiers and highly respected and sitting
under special leaves or eating only
the fattest of the dead and starting to vote
and starting to be corrupt for in the *Endings*

you can't help it, you are a true prisoner
this time, you run away from the Book
and the Fat Thumb, you go back to Sicily
and eat a mixed grill seafood smeared in lemon
or take a bus from Pittsburgh to Philadelphia
for four and a quarter and tell the fattest lamb
who's piling up wood for your own fire in some
sweet by-and-by if he's not careful you'll eat *him*
with coarse black pepper and fresh rosemary
for there are proofs and Karl Stirner from Easton
in Pennsylvania has by his own dour reckoning
only two more years at most though what he says
is twenty-four months, which sounds much shorter, and he is
in love with Grandma Moses, and what we call "Homer"
would reference Karl's strength by how he shot
up the rope, and threw the stone, and lifted
a piano once with his bald friend, so read
the Russians again, and breathe slowly, and try
the words to the song that I've been humming and touch
your left wrist to slow time down and kiss
the person sitting beside you to get ready.

Day of Grief

I was forcing a wasp to the top of a window
where there was some sky and there were tiger lilies
outside just to love him or maybe only
simply a kiss for he was hurrying home
to fight a broom and I was trying to open
a door with one hand while the other was swinging
tomatoes, and you could even smell the corn
for corn travels by wind and there was the first
hint of cold and dark though it was nothing
compared to what would come, and someone should mark
the day, I think it was August 20th, and
that should be the day of grief for grief
begins then and the corn man starts to shiver
and crows too and dogs who hate the wind
though grief would come later and it was a relief
to know I wasn't alone, but be as it may,
since it was cold and dark I found myself singing
the brilliant love songs of my other religion.

Why Anger Like That?

If for no other reason than that their shoes were black
and their soles were made of hard chewing gum
or that they made a deaf man's life miserable,
or for no other reason than that they made him remember
Little Russia where the whole city didn't speak English
and there were fifteen horns and twenty strings going north
and south between one tree-lined street and another,
and no other reason given than that they killed
their firstborn sons; and one time someone tried to
introduce into the diet charred birds on sticks,
and one time it rained so hard that all three rivers
became a lake and fish swam by on Water Street
across from the restaurant and a murder of cats
stood by to watch and, time to time, to stab
and pull the bleeding bodies from the water
in answer to your question since you're the fourth
person to ask, nor is there any issue
concerning the universes, and I've found the
strongest proponents live in old trailer courts
and argue around the spigots—you know me—
and I should be burying a steel box in the mud
by this time so you who live differently can stir
the dust and make a few things out for it's you I

love, I got it from Auden, I got it from a saint
you'd never recognize who lay drenched through and through
from the meadow he slept all night in waiting for morning.

Droit de Faim

Once I was a postwar doctoral student
eating a sandwich on the sly in one of the
nethermost aisles of an empty superette
on Broadway near 100th in the days of
unchecked books and I could cut my bread
and put on mayonnaise in a tenth of a second
and eat while walking in the direction of
the glass door, and though it's hard to explain
except in terms of hunger, or you might say
"droit de faim," though I would have said I was
St. John and I was in an El Greco painting
creating a world and I would have stuck to my story
even if I was slapped on the back of the neck
on the way to number this or that for I was
stubborn as the rind that covered the meat
or as the hardened skin of calf tongue stuck
in my throat I reached my fingers down to
carefully pull away from the windpipe it must have
wrapped itself around so I could breath
again after almost a minute and thus continue
forty-six more years, or let's say forty-
five and counting, in a world I adored

on a crowded hillside on the Delaware
inside a converted 1840s schoolhouse,
and there were other brutal happenings.

1946

One hand was holding the rail and one hand
was pushed up to the middle of his back
as if it were growing there, and he was disastrous
from looking too much backwards and from loving
slums too much, including the beans he ate
and the ketchup he spiced them with; and there were musicians
busting violins and bashing trombones
who also loved the slums and they had hands
too growing on their backs nor was there a suit
to fit them or a sweater and even their heads
were turned backwards, mostly because of the rivers
they once swam in and mostly because they tossed
their girlfriends over their heads or under their legs
in someone's small enlightened living room
or at Tom's Bar where beer was still a nickle,
before they raised everything to a dime,
including doughnuts and coffee and subway fares,
ruining our lives—the bastards—it almost killed us.

Bio III

I will go down in history without a hotel
for I have been dispersed, though what I wanted
was nothing, a box for my mail, a key,
an easy chair and a floor lamp with tufted string,
a coffee shop with access inside and outside
next to the lobby with a redheaded waitress.

I was waylaid, given what I was, by
2,000 books and a Plymouth station wagon
thirty feet long and easily twelve years old
that I could carry a piano in and park
anywhere I wanted, given the year then.

And I had a bench where I could think it through
when there were two seconds of silence in between
the delivery trucks, before my coffee got cold
and the crumbs on my lip were gobbled up by sparrows
catty-corner from Saint Andrew's Episcopal
where there is opera music four times a year
and you put clothes on the porch to give to the poor
—if I could compare one life to another—
though what I loved always got in the way.

Lowness

It was me who took a small white Fiat
out of my briefcase to let it breathe and after
a second started it by gathering speed
with my left foot and hopping into the seat and
giving it gas, as I remember, and driving or
pushing it into a Rolls-Royce garage in Edison
to get it repaired which I think compares to riding
a donkey into St. Johns or a scooter into
the great lobby of Temple Emanuel,
which partly explains but I don't understand it
and I'm embarrassed on the donkey's back
holding onto his mane or running beside that
scooter and hopping on on 5th Avenue
for I mean it and don't mean it though more likely
I would do either, I would do both, for I am a
spy on myself and it's no little thing
forgiving bastards, and loving lowness, and driving
a Fiat 500, 300 pounds, alongside
a giant truck for the sake of a little decency.